AKWAABA

AKWAABA
A Taste of Ghana

Recipes from the African Gold Coast

Sandra Amoako

Akwaaba: A Taste of Ghana
Recipes from the African Gold Coast

Printed in the United States of America
First Edition

This book was published by: Alikobooks

AliKoBooKs
491 Baltimore Pike, # 447
Springfield, PA 19064.
Email: info@alikobooks.com

PHOTOGRAPHY by Bako Photography[bakoko1@hotmail.com]

ISBN: 978-09825249-0-9

Library of Congress Control Number: 2009907621

This book uses U.S. cup measurements.

For more information, visit www.alikobooks.com

Contents

To my Dad

In loving memory
Rest in peace.

GHANA

"**GHANA** is a country located on the west coast of Africa. It is bordered on the north by Burkina Faso, on the east by Togo, on the south by the Atlantic Ocean, and on the west by Côte d'Ivoire (Ivory Coast). Accra is the capital and largest city of Ghana. It is located on the southeastern coast of Ghana.

Formerly a British colony, Ghana was known as the Gold Coast and was led to independence by Dr. Kwame Nkrumah on the 6th of March, 1957. Ghana became the first black nation in sub-Saharan Africa to achieve independence from colonial rule.

The country is named after the ancient empire of Ghana, from which the ancestors of the inhabitants of the present country are thought to have migrated.

Population

The population of Ghana is divided into 75 ethnic groups.

The most densely populated parts of the country are the coastal areas, the Ashanti region, and the two principal cities, Accra and Kumasi.

About 70 percent of the total population lives in the southern half of the country. The most numerous peoples are the coastal Fanti, and the Ashanti, who live in central Ghana, both of whom belong to the Akan family. The Accra plains are inhabited by the Ga-Adangbe. Most of the inhabitants in the northern region belong to the Moshi-Dagomba or to the Gonja group.*

Language

English is the official language of Ghana and is used in schools in addition to nine other local languages. The most widely spoken local languages are Ga, Dagomba, Akan and Ewe.

Religion

Traditional religion accounts for two-fifths of the population. The Christian population also accounts for two-fifths of the total population and includes Roman Catholics, Baptist, Protestants, etc. The Muslim population (12 percent of the total) is located chiefly in the northern part of the country."

*For more information on Ghana and what you need in order to visit Ghana, please visit www.ghanaembassy.org.

ACKNOWLEDGMENTS

I would like to thank my mother, Hannah and my aunt, Aunty Alice. There were some recipes that I needed some "brushing up" on and some that I had forgotten and so thank you for helping me with my "research".

Thanks to my friends, Akua, Amma, Amira and my sister Josephine ...thanks for the feedback!

Thanks to you! Thank you for reading my book. I hope you and your family enjoy these wonderful recipes and that they offer you a little piece of the vast culture that Ghana has to offer. I hope you will be inspired and perhaps take a trip to Ghana soon!

Most importantly, I would like to thank God for giving me the will and courage to start this adventure. This wonderful journey started two years ago with a lot of recipe testing, writing down recipes and testing recipes again and I hope it continues for a long time. It is always easy to talk about your dreams but it takes effort to make your dreams a success and I am grateful that I was empowered by my faith, my heart, my fears, my friends, my family and God to succeed. Thank you.

Enjoy!

INTRODUCTION

AS a native of Ghana who has lived overseas for many years, I still get to cook and enjoy some of the many traditional and modern cuisines I enjoyed when I lived in Ghana. However, there are always those foods that you may not have time to prepare or have simply forgotten how to prepare...the foods we used to eat "back home". These are some of the reasons that inspired me to write this cookbook.

What I hope to bring to you in this book is a gateway, not just to the great rich textures of some of the common, traditional recipes from Ghana, but also recipes that have been adapted into Ghanaian pallets by the wonderful and growing cultural diversity in Ghana.

Ghana is divided into many regions and each region has its specific recipes. However, the recipes I will be sharing with you are a compilation of some of the everyday cuisine that I grew up enjoying and that many Ghanaians enjoy on a daily basis. The recipes will range from breakfast porridge to soups to stews to everyday staples to desserts, pastries and much more.

Soups are one of the main components in Ghanaian cuisine and depending on which area you are visiting, you will get to taste the different kinds of soups. The soups in this book include peanut soup, which is one of the most well known soups from Ghana. Soups are normally eaten with staples such as rice and fufu.

For many years, I encountered people from all backgrounds who proclaimed their love for Ghanaian cuisine and their want to learn how to prepare such dishes. With not many Ghanaian cookbooks available, I was inspired and determined to provide a cookbook dedicated to authentic recipes from the Gold Coast (colonial name for Ghana) that anyone could prepare and enjoy.

These are all easy, step-by-step guidelines for anyone who has ever wanted to try something new or something forgotten. All ingredients being used are easily accessible, no matter what continent you live on. Akwaaba, from the AKAN language (one of the spoken dialects in Ghana) means welcome. Therefore, I welcome you to some of the wonderful tastes from Ghana and I hope that you enjoy these mouth-watering gateways to the Ghanaian culture and beyond.

Ghanaian people are known as one of the friendliest people and I hope that these recipes will entice you to take a trip to Ghana and experience the now familiar cuisine and friendly nation!

Akwaaba!

LIST OF ILLUSTRATIONS

YOUR GHANAIAN PANTRY

THESE are some of the ingredients you should always have available in your pantry for the many Ghanaian dishes you will be preparing.

- white onions - always keep them in the fridge so they will last longer
- ginger- when not in use, peel the ginger, put in a plastic bag and put in the freezer until needed. They only need a few minutes to thaw. In the recipes, a *"small-sized ginger root" is about 1 ½ inches long and ½ inch wide. A "medium-sized" ginger root is about 2 ½ inches long and 1 inch wide.* The amount of ginger in a meal really depends on your own preference so you can use more or less in a recipe.
- red peppers (habanero / serrano) - when not in use, put in plastic bag and put in the freezer until needed.
- canned tomato puree
- fresh tomatoes
- canned tomato paste
- Maggi cubes - always have the original versions, the shrimp versions and the chicken versions
- powdered red pepper - you can buy this at your local African grocery store
- nutmeg powder
- all-purpose white flour
- distilled white vinegar
- vegetable oil -
- white rice (long-grain or basmati) - this is a staple in a lot of dishes so always have some available
- iodized salt
- palm oil - you can find this at your local African grocery store [1]

[1] Visit www.africanbizbyzip.com to search for an African grocery store near you.

HELPFUL UTENSILS

THESE are some of the utensils needed for everyday Ghanaian cooking.

- Frying pan / skillet
- 5-quart pot - for cooking stews / sauces
- 6 to 8-quart stock pot - for cooking soups
- grater - to grate ginger, etc
- knives
- blender
- cutting board
- aluminum foil
- sieve - a small one and a large one
- long, wooden spoon
- long, stainless steel spoon - for cooking sauces and soups

BREAKFAST

RICE PUDDING

Makes 4 servings

Ingredients

- 1 cup of rice
- 1 can of evaporated milk (170g)
- ½ cup of sugar
- 4 cups of water

Preparation

1. Add the water into a cooking pot and place on the stove
2. Add the sugar and stir until most have dissolved
3. Add the rice to the sugar water
4. Let rice cook on low heat for 40 minutes
5. Pour in your desired amount of evaporated milk and stir
6. Pour rice pudding in serving bowls
7. Enjoy!

Helpful Hints and more:

- For a creamier rice pudding, mix 3 ½ cups of water with the entire can of evaporated and use that to boil the rice.
- Cook the rice on low heat so the rice will absorb the water. If you cook the rice on medium or high heat, it will turn out as regular cooked rice and not rice porridge.
- Use less or more sugar if desired.
- Use jasmine or long-grain rice for this recipe.
- ALWAYS wash rice before cooking it.
- Rice pudding, in Ghana, is a breakfast dish normally accompanied with tea bread or sugar bread.

Fun Fact

Ghana was a British colony

FRIED SWEET BREAD

Makes 4 servings

Ingredients

- 8 thick slices of sweet bread
- salted butter (at room temperature)

Preparation

1. Thoroughly butter both sides of each slice of bread
2. Heat your frying pan on medium heat for 3 minutes
3. Place slice of bread into pan and let “fry” for 1 minute until golden and brown
4. Flip bread onto “uncooked” side and let sizzle for 1 minute
5. Repeat steps 3 and 4 with remaining buttered slices

Helpful hints and more:

- Do not cut your slices too thin! Pre-sliced sweet bread is also available to buy at some African grocery stores.
- Only use sweet bread for this recipe as it has a unique taste and texture.
- Sweet bread is also known as sugar bread.
- Two slices per person is just an assumption...fry as many slices as you want!
- Butter is always better to fry with than margarine!
- This goes well with hot chocolate or tea
- If you feel like it, add some scrambled eggs to the plate!
- You can find sugar / sweet bread at your local African grocery store - visit www.africanbizbyzip.com to find an African grocery store near you.
- Enjoy!

Fun Fact

Ghana used to be called the Gold Coast

KOKO (CORNMEAL PORRIDGE)

Makes 4 servings

Ingredients

- 1 cup of fermented corn flour paste
- sugar (to taste)
- 1 can of evaporated milk (170g)
- 3 cups of warm water

Preparation

1. Place the fermented corn paste in a cooking pot
2. Add 3 cups of warm water
3. Stir until all the solids have dissolved
4. Place liquid porridge mix on a medium heat stove and cook for 10-15 minutes
5. Stir porridge as it cooks
6. Pour porridge into serving bowls
7. Add in some evaporated milk and sugar
8. Enjoy with some sweet bread

Helpful Hints and more:

- This is another common breakfast in Ghana.
- It is normally accompanied with some tea bread or sweet bread.
- You can find the frozen fermented cornmeal in the frozen food aisle at your local African store.
- If you cannot find it, you can also use the instant koko powder but it's always best to use the actual fermented corn meal.
- Adjust the sugar and milk according to your taste!
- For a thicker porridge, use less water (about ½ cup less water)
- For a lighter porridge, use more water (about ½ cup more water)
- Don't skimp on the evaporated milk...the more the better.
- Visit www.africanbizbyzip.com to find an African grocery store near you.

Fun Fact

Gold Coast gained independence on March 6th 1957 and was renamed Ghana

PANCAKES

Makes 4 servings

Ingredients

- 2 cups all-purpose flour
- 2 eggs
- ½ cup sugar
- 16 oz milk
- 2 tablespoons of nutmeg powder
- margarine or salted butter - for frying

Preparation

1. Beat eggs and milk together until you have an even consistency
2. In another bowl, mix sugar, flour and nutmeg
3. Slowly add egg mixture to flour and mix well until you have a smooth texture
4. Heat up frying pan on medium heat and base with butter or margarine
5. Pour some pancake batter and fry each side for about 2 minutes
6. Serve with honey(optional)
7. Repeat step 5 with remaining pancake batter

Helpful hints and more:

- Adding nutmeg gives the pancakes a great taste!
- I like to use 2% milk instead of whole milk.
- Instead of using fresh milk, you can mix a small can (170g) of evaporated milk with enough water to bring volume to 16oz.
- When pouring batter, I like to use a "1/4 cup" measuring cup- it gives you nice thin pancakes
- When frying the pancake, swirl the batter around in the pan so you get thin pancakes... almost like crepes.
- If you will be using syrup or honey, you do not have to add sugar to the batter.
- It's always better with honey!
- If however, you will be eating the pancakes without syrup, then add ½ cup sugar.

Fun Fact

The capital of Ghana is Accra

APPETIZERS

KÉLÉ WÉLÉ (SPICY FRIED, RIPE PLANTAINS)

Makes 4 servings

Ingredients

- 4 ripe plantains (yellow skin, firm)
- 2 medium ginger roots (2 ½ inches long & 1 inch wide)
- 4 red Serrano peppers
- 5 cups of oil (vegetable or coconut)
- 1 tablespoon of salt

Preparation

1. Wash and peel plantains
2. Cut across horizontally and dice plantains, wash and place them in a bowl
3. Peel ginger and puree, with the red peppers, in a food processor
4. Add the salt to pureed spice
5. Add spice mixture to diced plantains
6. Let marinate for 30 minutes
7. Pour oil in a pot and heat on medium-high for 5 - 7 minutes
8. Slowly add some plantains and let fry for 6 - 8 minutes until golden brown
9. Remove cooked kelé wélé and place on sheet of paper towel
10. Repeat steps 8 and 9 with remaining plantains

Helpful hints and more:

- Make sure plantains are ripe. You will be able to tell by its yellow skin.
- Make sure the oil is heated before frying. You can test by cutting a very small piece of plantain and placing in the oil. If you see a lot of tiny bubbles around the plantain, then the oil is hot enough.
- If you do not have fresh ginger root, you can always use store-ready ginger paste. Do not use ginger powder!!
- If you cannot find Serrano peppers, you can use any chili pepper of your choice.
- If you do not want your kelé wélé too spicy, you can always adjust the amount of pepper you marinate the plantains in.
- You can use either vegetable oil or coconut oil. To vary the taste of the kelé wélé,, I like to fry it in coconut oil every now and then.
- Line your sheet or bowl with paper towel so that excess oil from the kelé wélé can be absorbed before serving.
- For an extra "melt-in-your-mouth", munch the kelé wélé with some roasted peanuts. It makes a killer combination. Yummmmy!

Fun Fact

There are 10 regions in Ghana

TATALÉ (PLANTAIN CAKES)

Makes 4 servings

Ingredients

- 4 over ripe plantains (very soft)
- 1 medium ginger root (2 ½ inches long & 1 inch wide)
- 1 Habanero pepper
- 2/3 cup all-purpose flour
- 4 cups of vegetable oil (for frying)
- 2 small white onions

Preparation

1. Peel and mash plantain until texture has even consistency
2. Blend onions, peppers and ginger in a food processor
3. Add blended spices to mashed plantains and mix well
4. Add flour slowly to mashed plantains to bind the mixture
5. Let marinate for 30 - 40 minutes
6. Pour oil in a pot and heat on medium high for 5 to 7 minutes
7. Use a medium-sized ladle to scoop some plantain mixture into hot oil
8. Fry each side for 3 minutes or until golden brown
9. Remove cooked tatalé and place on sheet
10. Repeat steps 7,8,9 with remaining plantain mix

Helpful Hints and more:

- If you do not want to peel and puree ginger root, you can always use store-ready ginger paste
- You can also use red pepper powder for your marinade.
- When placing mixture in oil, use a ladle or ice-cream scoop with lever to get equal size tatalés.
- Depending on how big your pot is, you can fry a few tatalés at the same time
- Make sure you use over ripe plantains - the outer skin should be turning black or should be almost black. It has to be very soft in order to mash it.
- For a smoother texture, you can use an electric hand-mixer to mash the plantains
- I love this recipe! You can eat tatalé as a snack or you can combine it with some beans stew (upcoming chapter)and create a meal!

Fun Fact

There are 4 linguistic groups in Ghana: Akan, Ga, Mole-Dagbani, Ewe

FRIED YAMS WITH RED PEPPER SAUCE

Makes 4 servings

Ingredients

- ½ a tuber of Ghana yam (imported)
- 2 tablespoons of salt
- 4 cups of oil (for frying)
- 3 Serrano peppers
- 2 medium-sized tomatoes
- 2 small white onions

Preparations

YAM

1. Wash and peel skin off the yam
2. Wash peeled yam and cut in medium-sized strips
3. Place yam in a water-filled bowl and add 1 tablespoon of salt
4. In a cooking pot, heat oil on medium-high heat for 5 -7 minutes
5. Place yam strips in hot oil and let fry for 10 - 12 minutes (until golden yellow)
6. Place on sheet or plate lined with paper towel (to drain excess oil)

PEPPER SAUCE

7. Place peppers, tomatoes, onions and 1 tablespoon of salt in a food processor
8. Grind till you get smooth texture

Helpful Hints and more:

- There are different types of yams. Make sure you get the yam (see glossary) specific to this recipe.
- You can buy Ghanaian yam from an African grocery store. Visit www.africanbizbyzip.com to find an African grocery store near you. .
- You can also eat the fried yams with black pepper sauce (shitor - later chapter).
- This pepper sauce is also eaten with kenkey and fried fish (later chapters)

Fun Fact

Ghana is bordered by Togo on the east and Cote D'Ivoire on the west

SALAD

Makes 4 servings

Ingredients

- 2 heads of Romaine lettuce
- 4 large eggs
- 1 medium red onion
- 1 large cucumber
- 2 cups of cherry tomatoes
- 4 canned sardines (in oil)
- 1 can of baked beans (vegetarian version)
- Heinz salad cream (1/4 of the bottle)
- 1 cup of white vinegar

Preparation

1. Boil eggs for 12-15 minutes until well cooked
2. Wash and cut onion into rings;
3. Wash and cut cucumbers into thin slices
4. Wash, dry and chop salad leaves and place in a salad bowl
5. Place onion rings and cucumber slices in a separate bowl and marinate contents in vinegar for 5 minutes
6. Remove contents from vinegar solution and add to salad leaves
7. Mash (slightly) sardines and add to salad bowl (include oil from 1 can)
8. Pour baked beans onto salad
9. Pour salad cream onto salad and mix all ingredients thoroughly
10. Peel and cut eggs into half-slices and place on top of mixed salad

Helpful hints and more:

- When using baked beans, you can use any brand of vegetarian baked beans.
- You can get the Heinz salad cream from African grocery store - visit www.africanbizbyzip.com to find an African grocery store near you.
- When buying canned sardines, make sure you get the sardines in oil as it gives the salad extra flavor!
- This recipe recommends pouring about 1/4 of the bottle of the Heinz salad cream but you can use more for your salad if you prefer.
- You can eat this salad on its own but we normally eat it with a dish such as Jollof.

Fun Fact

Ghana is similar in size to Great Britain

AVOCADO AND PEANUT DRESSING

Makes 6 - 8 servings

Ingredients:

- 4 ripe avocados
- 1 large lemon
- 4 tablespoons of freshly ground peanut paste or peanut butter
- 1 ½ teaspoons of paprika powder
- 1 teaspoon of cinnamon powder

Preparation:

1. Peel and dice the avocados and place in a bowl
2. Cut lemon in half and squeeze juice on diced avocados
3. Slightly toss the avocados so they are thoroughly covered with the lemon juice
4. Place the avocados on a serving plate
5. Place peanut paste, paprika and cinnamon in a food processor and puree for 10 seconds
6. Garnish each diced avocado with some of the spicy peanut mix
7. Cool in refrigerator till ready to serve.

Helpful Hints and more:

- When choosing the avocados, make sure they are ripe AND firm.
- Place a toothpick in each diced avocado for easy handling.
- Squeezing the lemon juice on the avocados is very important as it gives it a great taste and also prevents it from turning brown.
- If you do not have a food processor, you can mix the peanut paste and spice in a small bowl with a (wooden) spoon.
- This makes a great appetizer or a great snack!

Fun Fact

Ghana is similar in size to the U.S. State of Oregon

FISH BALLS

Makes 4 servings

Ingredients:

- 16 oz Tilapia fillet (boneless)
- 1/8 cup salted butter (room temperature)
- 1/4 cup all-purpose flour
- ½ teaspoon of salt
- 1 tablespoon of white pepper
- lemon juice (from ½ a lemon)
- 1/4 cup of chopped parsley
- 1 small white onion (finely chopped)
- 1 garlic clove (finely chopped)
- 1 crushed Maggi cube (shrimp flavor)
- 2 eggs (1 for dipping, 1 for mixing)
- bread crumbs
- oil (for frying)

Preparation:

- Bake the Tilapia fillet at 450F for 14 - 15 minutes, then let cool for about 2 minutes.
- Flake the cooked Tilapia meat in a bowl.
- Separate egg whites and yolk from 1 egg and place each in separate bowls and place on the side.
- In a small cup, beat the other egg.
- Place the bread crumbs in another bowl and place on the side.
- Add the white pepper, chopped parsley, finely chopped onions and garlic to flaked fish and mix well
- Then add in the crushed Maggi cube, salt, butter, flour, beaten egg and lemon juice
- Mix all ingredients well and shape fish mixture into balls
- Dip each fish ball into the egg white and then dip in the bowl of bread crumbs
- Heat oil on medium-high heat for 5-7 minutes
- Fry the fish balls for 4 - 5 minutes on each side until golden brown.

Helpful Hints and more:

- You can use any type of fish fillet (e.g.: tilapia, flounder) with this recipe.
- With this recipe, you can use packaged fish fillet or fresh fish fillet from your grocery.
- Instead of adding flour to the fish mix, you can use 1 small boiled potato.
- You can also mold the fish mixture into fish cakes instead of fish balls. When cooking your fish fillet, bake in the oven at 450F for 9-10 minutes (if thawed) and 14-15 minutes (if frozen).
- When frying the fish, fill your frying pot halfway with vegetable oil. If you deep fry the fish balls, just fry them for about 5 minutes total instead of 4 minutes on each side.
- If you cannot find any Maggi cubes, you can use any seafood flavored bouillon cube.
- You can also fry the fish balls without dipping them in the egg white and bread crumbs. Another coating for the fish balls would be to dip them in the egg white and then some flour.
- You can also mix some flour and water to create a batter, then dip the fish balls in before frying.

Fun Fact

Ghana's local time is the Greenwich Mean Time (GMT)

YAM BALLS

Makes 4 - 6 servings

Ingredients

- 1/4 tuber of Ghana yam
- 1 medium white onion (diced)
- 1/4 cup of chopped parsley
- ½ teaspoon of white pepper
- 1 large egg
- 1 teaspoon of salt
- 1/4 cup flour

Preparation

1. Wash, peel and cut the yam into several pieces then boil yam for 30 minutes
2. Dice the onion
3. Mash boiled yam with a big spoon or food processor then add diced onions, parsley, white pepper and salt; then place mixture in a bowl
4. Beat egg and add to seasoned, mashed yam until evenly mixed
5. Scoop yam mixture and shape into balls
6. Roll yam balls in the flour until evenly coated
7. Heat some oil on medium-high heat for 5 - 7 minutes until hot
8. Fry the yam balls for 4- 5 minutes on each side until golden brown.

Helpful hints and more:

- You can add other seasonings (e.g. cumin, garlic) of your choice
- For a crunchy taste, substitute the flour with bread crumbs
- There are different types of yam, so make sure to get the Ghana yam from an African store- visit www.africanbizbyzip.com to find an African grocery store near you.
- You can use a small ice cream scoop to scoop yam mixture into the frying oil
- Place gas mark on medium-high heat but make sure the oil is heated (5 - 10 minutes) before frying.

Fun Fact

People from Ghana are called Ghanaians

SOUPS

PEANUT SOUP WITH SKINLESS, BONELESS CHICKEN BREASTS

Makes 6 - 8 servings

Ingredients

- 4 large tablespoon scoops of peanut butter
- 6 cups of water
- 4 medium-sized tomatoes
- 1(peeled) medium-sized, ginger root (2 ½ inches long & 1 inch wide)
- 1 Habanero pepper
- 3 lbs of skinless, boneless chicken breast
- 1/8 cup vegetable oil
- 1 large white onion
- salt (to taste)

Preparation

1. Wash and dice chicken breasts
2. Place diced chicken, with 1 cup of water, in cooking pot and steam for 25 minutes
3. Place cooked chicken and its broth in a bowl and cover
4. Place 6 cups of hot water and 4 tablespoon scoops of peanut butter in blender
5. Blend until you get smooth texture
6. Wash onion and cut into 2 pieces(3/4 piece; 1/4 piece) while chicken is cooking ; dice the 1/4 piece of the onion
7. Heat oil in a cooking pot and add diced onions; let them fry for 2 minutes
8. Pour peanut liquid into pot and let boil for about 15 minutes
9. Blend tomatoes, undiced onion, pepper and ginger and pour into cooking pot
10. Let simmer on medium heat for 30 minutes
11. Then add cooked chicken and 4 tablespoons of chicken broth to soup
12. Cover soup and let simmer on low heat for about 30 -40 minutes
13. Add salt to taste.

Helpful hints and more:

- You can use regular peanut butter or organic, unsweetened peanut butter.
- Use an actual tablespoon and not a "measuring tablespoon" when scooping out peanut butter
- When scooping the peanut butter, scoop a good size of peanut butter; do not scoop a level tablespoon of peanut butter.
- If you do not have fresh ginger root, use can use 3- 4 teaspoons ginger paste...never ginger powder!
- If you are a vegetarian, you can replace the chicken with vegetables such as cauliflower, baby carrots, etc.
- If you are not into chicken, you can substitute with other meats such as beef or fish.
- Add some salt to the soup right before adding the cooked chicken and after the soup is done.
- You can enjoy this soup on its own or on top of some boiled rice, with some rice balls (later chapter) or with some fufu (later chapter)

Fun Fact

The official language of Ghana is English

PEANUT SOUP WITH CHICKEN DRUMSTICKS (ALTERNATE METHOD)

Makes 6 - 8 servings

Ingredients

- 4 large tablespoon scoops of peanut butter
- 6 cups of water
- 4 medium-sized tomatoes
- 1 medium peeled ginger root (2 ½ inches long & 1 inch wide)
- 1 orange Habanero pepper
- 3 lbs of chicken drumsticks
- 2 large white onions
- 1 Maggi cube (chicken flavor)
- salt (to taste)

Preparation

1. Wash chicken and place in a cooking pot
2. Blend the onions and peeled ginger and pour over drumsticks
3. Pour 6 cups of water to chicken and let cook for 25 - 30 minutes
4. Place 4 tablespoon scoops of peanut butter and 1 cup of chicken broth (from cooking pot) in blender
5. Blend until you get smooth peanut butter liquid
6. Add peanut butter liquid into the cooking pot and stir
7. Let boil for another 10 minutes
8. Blend tomatoes, pepper and ½ cup of boiling peanut butter liquid and pour into cooking pot
9. Cover soup and let simmer on low heat for 40- 50 minutes
10. Add salt to taste.

Helpful hints and more:

- You can use regular peanut butter or organic, unsweetened peanut butter.
- **Use an actual tablespoon** and not a "measuring tablespoon" when scooping out peanut butter
- Add about 1/4 cup of water when blending the onions and ginger...makes blending easier
- Add some salt to the soup right before adding the cooked chicken and after the soup is done.
- Make sure the chicken is thoroughly cooked before adding the peanut butter liquid
- You can also crush and add one chicken Maggi cube to the soup to enhance the soup's taste. If you feel you still need to add some salt later, then do so.
- You can enjoy this soup on its own or on top of some boiled rice, with some rice balls (later chapter) or with some fufu (later chapter)

Fun Fact

Ghana is one of the major producers of gold in the world

"LIGHT" SOUP (PEPPER SOUP)

Makes 6 - 8 servings

Ingredients

- 2 lbs fish (dried or steamed)
- 1 lb lean beef
- 1 medium-sized white onion
- 4 large tomatoes
- 2 Habanero peppers
- 2 Maggi cubes (shrimp flavor)
- 2 tablespoons of salt
- 1 medium ginger root, peeled (2 ½ inches long & 1 inch wide)
- 2 garden eggs (eggplant)

Preparation

1. Wash and cut beef into bite-size cubes and place in cooking pot
2. Dice the onion and add, with salt and crushed maggi cubes, to the beef
3. Add ½ cup of water and steam meat for 25 minutes on medium-high heat
4. Then add 5 cups of water to the cooked beef and bring to boil
5. In separate pot (*while meat is cooking*), boil the garden eggs and peppers for 10 minutes
6. Blend boiled garden eggs, Habanero peppers, tomatoes and the ginger root
7. Add blended mix to the meat and let cook for 20 minutes on medium heat
8. Then add fish to simmering soup
9. Let soup simmer for 30 minutes on low heat
10. Add salt to taste

Helpful Hints and more:

- Meat Options - you can substitute the fish with beef or use both.
- You can use any fish such as Tilapia, cod or haddock - either dried or freshly steamed.
- Adjust salt as you cook the soup as adding blended ingredients will dilute taste.
- When blending the tomatoes, eggplant, etc., adding some liquid from the cooking pot to the blender makes it easier to puree those ingredients.
- If you cannot find Maggi cubes you can use any bouillon cube - in this case, make sure it's shrimp or seafood flavor.
- If you cannot find garden eggs, you can use one large eggplant - peel the skin before boiling, then puree as you would in the recipe.
- If you do not have any eggplant whilst making this recipe, you can also use two table-spoons of tomato paste - add it to the steamed meat, just before adding the 5 cups of water.
- You can enjoy this soup by itself, with fufu or on boiled rice or with rice balls.

Fun Fact

Diamond is one of Ghana's natural resources

SPINACH SOUP

Makes 6 - 8 servings

Ingredients

- 2 lbs fish (dried or steamed)
- 1 lb lean beef
- 1 medium white onion
- 4 large tomatoes
- 2 Habanero peppers
- 2 Maggi cubes (shrimp flavor)
- salt (to taste)
- 1 medium ginger root (2 ½ inches long & 1 inch wide)
- 2 garden eggs (eggplant)
- 2 bags of spinach (6 oz each)

Preparation

1. Wash and cut beef into bite-size cubes and place in cooking pot
2. Dice the onion and add, with salt and crushed maggi cubes, to the beef
3. Add ½ cup of water and steam meat for 25 minutes until cooked
4. Add 5 cups of water to meat and bring to boil
5. In separate pot (*while meat is cooking*), boil the garden eggs and peppers for 10 minutes
6. Blend boiled garden eggs, Habanero peppers, tomatoes and the peeled ginger root
7. Add blended mix to the meat and let cook on medium heat for 20 minutes
8. Add fish and let soup simmer for another10 minutes
9. Place the spinach and a 1 cup of the soup in a blender and puree
10. Pour liquid spinach into the soup
11. Let simmer for another 20 - 30 minutes on low heat.
12. Add salt to taste

Helpful Hints and more:

- Meat Options - you can substitute the fish with beef or use both.
- You can use any fish such as cod or haddock - either dried or freshly steamed.
- Adjust salt as you cook the soup as adding blended ingredients will dilute taste.
- When blending the tomatoes and other ingredients, it helps to add about ½ cup of water from the cooking pot to the blender.
- If you cannot find Maggi cubes (available at African grocery stores), you can use any bouillon cube - in this case, make sure it's shrimp or seafood flavor.
- If you cannot find garden eggs, you can use one large eggplant - peel the skin before boiling, then puree as you would in the recipe.
- If you do not have any eggplant whilst making this recipe, you can also use two table-spoons of tomato paste - add it to the steamed meat, just before adding the 5 cups of water.
- You can enjoy this soup by itself, with fufu or on boiled rice or with rice balls.
- If you cannot find fresh garden eggs, you can always use the canned variety (imported).

Fun Fact

Cocoa is one of Ghana's natural resources

PALM NUT SOUP

Makes 8 - 10 servings

Ingredients

- 1 can (800g) of palm nut paste
- 6 ½ cups of hot water
- 3 lbs of lean beef
- 1 tablespoon of red pepper powder
- 1 Habanero pepper
- 4 medium sized tomatoes
- 1 large white onion
- 1 tablespoon of salt (for cooking beef)
- salt (for soup - to taste)
- 1 medium ginger root (2 ½ inches long & 1 inch wide)

Preparation

1. Dice beef into bite-size cubes and place in a cooking pot
2. Dice onions and add to the meat
3. Add 1 tablespoon of salt, ½ cup of water and pepper powder to the meat
4. Cover cooking pot and steam meat on medium heat for 25 minutes until cooked
5. In a large bowl, mix can of palm nut paste and 6 ½ cups of hot water
6. Add palm nut mixture to cooked meat and cook for 20 minutes
7. Put the tomatoes, habanero pepper and the ginger root in a blender, puree and pour mix into the soup and stir.
8. Let soup simmer for 35 - 40 minutes on low heat
9. Add salt to taste.

Helpful hints and more:

- Adjust salt and spices to your taste.
- You can also include other meats such as fish and whole crabs to the soup. When using fish, add it a few minutes after adding the blended tomatoes.
- When mixing palm paste, amount of water should be 1 ½ times the amount of paste. Thus, once you pour the paste in a bowl, you can use the empty can to measure amount of water needed.
- When blending the tomatoes and other ingredients, it helps the process when you add a little liquid from the cooking pot to the blender.
- This soup is generally eaten with rice balls or fufu
- OUTSIDE THE BOX - to try something extra different: boil some black-eyed peas and place a few tablespoons in a bowl. Add some palm soup and peanut soup in the bowl and stir. Place some rice balls in the bowl and enjoy! It's a winning combination...let me know what you think!
- You can find palm nut paste at your local African grocery store - visit www.africanbiz-byzip.com to find an African grocery store near you.

Fun Fact

Electrical items in Ghana operate on 220/240 volts

STEWS & SAUCES

BEANS STEW

Makes 6 - 8 servings

Ingredients

- 2 cans (418g each) of Salmon (optional)
- 2 medium-sized white onions
- 8 large tomatoes *or* 1 can(29 oz) of tomato puree
- 2 teaspoons of red pepper powder
- 1 cup of vegetable oil
- ½ cup of Palm oil
- 2 cubes of Maggi Crevette (shrimp flavored bouillon cube)
- 1 lb of black-eyed peas
- 1 small -sized ginger root (1½ inch long & ½ inch wide)

Preparation

1. Rinse and soak peas in 8 cups of cold water and let stand overnight
2. Drain and rinse peas
3. Add 6 cups of hot water to rinsed peas and simmer on medium heat, with lid tilted, for 2 ½ hrs
4. Dice 1 onion and blend the other onion with the tomato puree and peeled ginger root
5. Heat vegetable oil on medium-high heat for about 5 - 7 minutes
6. Add diced onions and red pepper powder to heated oil and let simmer for 3 minutes
7. Add 1/4 cup of water to frying onions and let simmer for another 3 minutes
8. Add blended tomato mix to frying onions
9. Let sauce cook for 30 minutes on medium heat (stir every 15 minutes)
10. Add 1 cup of water to sauce and let it cook for another 20 minutes
11. Then stir in 1 teaspoon of salt and the 2 Maggi cubes
12. Add salmon (*optional*) and cooked beans to the cooking sauce and let simmer on low heat another 30 minutes
13. Add palm oil to cooked stew
14. Add salt to taste

Helpful Hints and more:

For a quick soak of the peas: rinse and sort peas in a pot. Add 8 cups of hot water and bring to rapid boil. Boil for about 2 -3 minutes. Drain soak water and rinse peas. Then add 6 cups of cold water to rinsed peas and simmer on medium heat for 2 hours.

- You can also cook the beans the day before and refrigerate for next day cooking.
- Start cooking sauce when beans have been boiling for about 1 ½ hours.
- Fully drain salmon of the liquid in the can before adding to the sauce.
- Always cover the cooking pot with a lid as the sauce can splatter as it cooks.
- This stew is great with fried, red plantains (this combo is also called red-red)
- It can also be mixed with moistened gari to make gari fotor (*later chapter*).
- If you cannot find Maggi cubes at your local African stores, you can substitute them with any bouillon cubes - visit www.africanbizbyzip.com to find a local African grocery store.
- For a vegetarian version, do not add the salmon!
- You can always substitute salmon with dried or smoked or steamed fish (haddock, cod, Tilapia).
- For a more spicy stew, you can always add more red pepper powder!
- This stew takes a long time to prepare so keep that in mind when trying this recipe ...some parts (cooking beans) can be prepared a day or two beforehand.

Fun Fact

The official currency of Ghana is the cedi (¢)

SPINACH STEW

Makes 6 -8 servings

Ingredients

- 2 bags(6oz each) of spinach
- 8 large tomatoes or 1 can (29 oz) of tomato puree
- 2 medium-sized white onions
- 1 lb lean beef - diced
- 20oz Tilapia fillet (steamed)
- ½ cup of palm oil
- ½ cup of vegetable oil
- 1 ½ teaspoon red pepper
- 1 Habanero pepper
- 1(grated) small-sized ginger root (1 ½ inches long & ½ inch wide)
- salt

Preparation

1. Heat vegetable oil and palm oil in cooking pot on medium heat for 3 minutes
2. Wash and dice one onion and fry in heated oil for 3 minutes
3. Add red pepper powder and grated ginger to frying onions and let simmer for 1 minute
4. Add 1/4 cup of water to frying onions and let simmer for another 3 minutes
5. Blend tomatoes, the other onion and habanero pepper and add to frying onions; let simmer for 10 minutes
6. Add 1 cup of water to the sauce and let it simmer on medium heat for 30 minutes
7. Meanwhile, dice and wash beef, season with salt, add 1/4 cup of water and steam for 20 minutes in another cooking pot
8. Add cooked meat and steamed Tilapia fillets to cooking sauce and let simmer on medium heat for 15 - 20 minutes
9. Wash spinach leaves and add to sauce
10. Let stew simmer for about 20 -25 minutes on medium-low heat until cooked
11. Add salt to taste

Helpful Hints and more:

- You do not have to add the beef to this stew but most definitely add some type of steamed or smoked fish to the stew.
- You can even use a combination of canned Salmon with the steamed Tilapia fillets instead of the beef.
- Always use palm oil...gives it the authentic taste
- You can also steam the spinach before adding it to the stew - place spinach in a sieve (with a lid) and place over a pot of boiling water for about 5 minutes.

Fun Fact

It is custom for children to be named after the day (Monday, Tuesday, etc) they were born

CHICKEN STEW

Makes 6 - 8 servings

Ingredients

- 1 29oz can of tomato puree or 8 large tomatoes
- 2 large white onions
- 1 Habanero pepper
- 1 small-sized ginger root (1 ½ inches long & ½ inch wide)
- 1 ½ cups of vegetable oil (for frying chicken)
- 1 cup of vegetable oil (for cooking the stew)
- 1 teaspoon nutmeg
- 1 tablespoon curry powder (optional)
- 3 lbs of chicken drumsticks / chicken thighs
- 2 Maggi cubes (chicken version)
- 1 tablespoon of chicken seasoning
- ½ cup of chicken stock (from boiled chicken)

Preparation

1. Dice one of the onions and place in a bowl
2. Blend other onion with the peeled ginger and habanero pepper until you get an even texture
3. Place chicken in a cooking pot and add the chicken seasoning, 4 tablespoons of the ginger-onion puree mix, 1 teaspoon of salt and 2 cups of water
4. Boil chicken over medium-high heat for 30 minutes until cooked.
5. In a separate frying pan, heat 1½ cups of vegetable oil on medium-high heat for 5 minutes
6. Place cooked chicken in the hot oil and fry for 3 minutes on each side until golden brown
7. Remove fried chicken from oil and place in a separate bowl or plate
8. Heat up 1 cup of oil in another cooking pot then fry diced onions for 3 minutes
9. Add the pepper powder, curry powder and nutmeg to the frying onions and let simmer for 1 minute.
10. Add tomato puree and remainder of ginger-onion mix and let cook for 20 minutes on medium heat
11. Add 2 cups of water to tomato puree and let simmer on medium heat for another 10 minutes
12. Add the chicken stock and mashed Maggi cubes to the stew and let simmer for another 10 minutes
13. Add fried chicken to the stew and let cook for 30 - 40 minutes on low heat.
14. Add salt to taste

Helpful hints and more:

- Adjust pepper powder according to your level of spiciness!
- You can also use skinless, boneless, chicken breasts cut into medium-size pieces for the stew.
- When blending the onions and other ingredients, it helps the process by adding a little water (½ cup) into the blender.
- Line the plate with some paper towel before placing fried chicken - it helps absorb some of the oil.
- After pouring in tomato puree from can, rinse the can with a little water(1/4 cup) and pour into the cooking pot - this allows you to not waste any of the tomato puree remaining in the can.
- Pour chicken and its stock in a bowl when cooked and re-use that cooking pot for the stew - this saves you using and therefore washing another cooking pot!

Fun Fact

Among the Akans, a child is named by the 8th day after birth

CORNED BEEF STEW

Makes 6 - 8 servings

Ingredients

- 1 29oz can of tomato puree or 8 large tomatoes
- 1 large white onion
- 1 tablespoon red pepper powder
- 1 small-sized ginger root (1 ½ inches long & ½ inch wide)
- 1 cup of vegetable oil
- 1 teaspoon nutmeg powder
- 2 cans of corned beef
- 2 Maggi cubes

Preparation

1. Cut onion in two and dice one-half of it
2. Place other half of the onion in a blender, add ginger, can of tomato puree and blend till you get an even texture
3. In separate pot, heat oil and fry diced onions for 3 minutes
4. Add pepper powder and nutmeg powder to fried onions and stir
5. Add blended tomato mix to the cooked onions and let simmer on medium heat for 20 minutes
6. Mash Maggi cubes and add to cooking pot
7. After 10 minutes, add corned beef to cooking sauce and let cook on medium-low heat for 30 minutes.
8. Add salt to taste

Helpful hints and more:

- Add salt after stew is cooked to avoid the sauce being too salty - the corned beef adds salt to the stew as well.
- Adjust pepper powder according to your level of spiciness!
- This goes great with boiled rice, boiled yams and even kenkey!
- This canned corned beef is totally different from the cured or boiled version of corned beef in making sandwiches!
- Get the corned beef from the canned meat aisle at your local grocery store!

Fun Fact

The first Ghanaian capital was Cape Coast then it was transferred to Accra

GARDEN EGG STEW

Makes 6 - 8 servings

Ingredients

- 9 garden eggs (eggplants)
- 8 large tomatoes or 1 can (29 oz) of tomato puree
- 2 large white onions
- 1 tablespoon of red pepper powder (imported)
- 1 Habanero pepper
- 1 teaspoon of nutmeg powder
- 1(grated) small ginger root (1 ½ inches long & ½ inch wide)
- ½ lb of fish (steamed)
- 1 cup of dried shrimp
- 1cup of palm oil
- salt (to taste)

Preparation

1. Boil the garden eggs for 12 - 15 minutes, then remove the skin and seeds
2. Dice the garden eggs and place in a bowl
3. Heat palm oil in a cooking pot for about 3 - 5 minutes on medium heat
4. Dice 1 onion and fry in heated palm oil for 3 minutes
5. Add pepper powder and nutmeg powder to frying onions and let simmer for 3 minutes
6. Add dried shrimp to the frying onions
7. Blend tomatoes, habanero pepper and the other onion and add to frying onions
8. Let sauce simmer for about 15 minutes on medium heat
9. Add 1 cup of water to sauce and let simmer for another 20 minutes
10. Then add the fish and diced garden eggs to sauce
11. Let the stew simmer for another 30 - 40 minutes on low heat
12. Add salt to taste

Helpful Hints and more:

- Garden egg is another name for eggplant
- It is called garden egg because of its eggshell color, size and shape... it looks like an egg!
- If you cannot find this kind of eggplant, you can buy the canned version in your local grocery store or African store or use any local eggplant at your grocery store or market
- If using a local type of eggplant, prepare it the same way as in this recipe - boil, then remove skin and seeds.
- You can use any fish of your choosing - Tilapia, cod, haddock (steamed or dried)
- This stew goes great with boiled yam, green or red plantains, rice and even boiled potatoes.
- If you are using canned diced tomatoes, you can add it straight to the heated oil and just blend the onion and habanero peppers.
- If you are using fresh tomatoes, you can opt to dice them instead of blending them with the onion and pepper.

Fun Fact

In the Eastern region, the Yam Festival is celebrated during the whole month of July

FISH STEW

Makes 6 - 8 servings

Ingredients:

- 1 29oz can of tomato puree or 8 large tomatoes
- 1 large white onion
- 1 tablespoon red pepper powder
- 1 small ginger root (1 ½ inches long & ½ inch wide)
- 1 cup of vegetable oil
- 1 teaspoon nutmeg powder
- 32 oz smoked fish (Tilapia, cod, haddock, etc)
- 2 Maggi crevettes (shrimp bouillon cubes)

Preparation

- Cut onion in half and dice one-half of it
- Place other half of onion in blender, add ginger, can of tomato puree and blend till you get an even texture
- In separate pot, heat oil on medium heat for 3 minutes and fry diced onions for 3 minutes
- Stir in pepper powder and nutmeg powder to frying onions and let sizzle for 3 minutes
- Add blended tomato mix to the frying onions and let simmer on medium heat for 20 minutes
- Add 3/4 cup of water and let sauce simmer for another 20 minutes
- Mash the Maggi cubes and stir into the stew
- After 5 minutes, add smoked fish to sauce and let cook on medium-low for 35 minutes.
- Add salt to taste

Helpful Hints and more:

- You can use any smoked or salted fish of your choice.
- You can also use canned salmon
- If you do not have Maggi cubes, you can always use a shrimp flavored bouillon cube.
- You can buy maggi cubes at your local African grocery store - visit www.africanbizbyzip.com to find an African grocery store near you.

Fun Fact

During the Yam Festival, there is a ban on activities like drumming, funerals and farming

OKRA STEW

Makes 6 - 8 servings

Ingredients

- 7 - 8 cups (2 lbs) of okra
- 8 large tomatoes or 1 can (29 oz) of tomato puree
- 2 medium size white onions
- 3 garden eggs / eggplants (boiled and diced)
- 1 lb lean beef
- 16oz of fish (dried or steamed)
- 2 tablespoons of dried shrimp powder
- 1 cup of palm oil
- 1 ½ teaspoon red pepper
- 1 (grated) small-sized ginger root (1 ½ inches long & ½ inch wide)
- salt

Preparation

1. Wash and dice 1 of the onions
2. Heat palm oil in cooking pot on medium heat for 3 - 5 minutes
3. Place diced onions in hot palm oil and fry for 3 minutes
4. Stir in red pepper powder and grated ginger to frying onions
5. Blend tomatoes and remaining onion and add to frying onions
6. Then stir in shrimp powder and ½ cup of water
7. Let sauce cook for 20 minutes on medium heat
8. Meanwhile, wash and dice beef, season with salt, add 1/4 cup of water and cook in separate pot for 20 minutes
9. Add cooked meat (and liquid stock) and fish to simmering sauce and let cook for 10 - 15 minutes
10. Wash and dice the okra and add, with diced garden eggs (eggplant), to cooking sauce
11. Let the stew simmer for about 30 minutes on medium-low heat
12. Add salt to taste.

Helpful Hints and more:

- If you are going to be using fresh tomatoes, buy them a day or two before cooking and store at room temperature for the best taste
- You can also use ready-to-use, frozen okra from your local grocery store
- If you cannot find garden eggs, you can use 2 large eggplants (locally grown).
- You can also use 1 can (29 oz) of diced tomatoes - you can add it straight to the cooking pot and just blend the onion and ginger.

Fun Fact

The Homowo Festival (August/ September) is celebrated by the Ga people

SHITOR (BLACK PEPPER SAUCE)

Makes 15 - 20 servings

Ingredients

- 1 ½ cups of ground, dried shrimp
- 2 cups of dried crayfish
- 5 tablespoons of red pepper powder
- 2 teaspoons of ginger (grated)
- 9 medium white onions
- 2 cans (6 oz each) of tomato paste
- 6 cups of vegetable oil
- 6 Maggi cubes (shrimp flavor; crushed)
- 4 teaspoons of salt

Preparation

1. Dice 1 onion
2. Blend the remaining onions
3. Pour the oil into the cooking pot and let heat up on medium-heat for 10 minutes
4. Add diced onions and let fry for about 2 minutes.
5. Stir in red pepper powder and grated ginger and let simmer for 1 minute
6. Add blended onions and tomato paste to the pot and let cook on medium heat for 30 minutes
7. Add the Maggi cubes to the sauce and let simmer for another 10 - 12 minutes.
8. Add ground shrimp and dried crayfish to the sauce and let cook on medium-low heat for 50 - 60 minutes until sauce is dark brown in color.
9. Add salt to taste (if needed)

Helpful Hints and more:

- Add salt after adding shrimp and dried fish and not before so as not to make the sauce too salty!
- For a spicier sauce, use 6 to 8 tablespoons of red pepper powder.
- You can use fresh crushed ginger or ginger powder.
- When blending the onions, add a little water(½ cup) in the blender for easy blending.
- You can get already ground, dried shrimp from your local African grocery store. If none is available, you can find dried shrimp from your local grocery store and grind in a food processor.
- You can also find bagged, dried crayfish at your local African grocery store.
- When storing the sauce, make sure there is plenty of oil in the storage containers - always divide sauce into separate containers. The oil helps preserve the sauce and gives it a long shelf life.
- Store unused sauce in the freezer.

Fun Fact

The Homowo Festival celebrates the plentiful harvest and makes fun of hunger

MEATS

KEBAB

Makes 4 servings

Ingredients

- 2 lbs of lean beef (top sirloin)
- 2 large white onions
- 1 cup of kebab pepper (imported)
- vegetable oil
- 8 wooden skewer sticks
- 1 tablespoon of salt

Preparation

1. Soak sticks in water for about 1 hour to prevent them from burning
2. Preheat oven to 450F or your grill to high heat
3. Dice beef in bite size cubes (1 inch cubes)
4. Cut each onion in 4 and peel off layers
5. Place diced beef and onions in a bowl and add salt and kebab pepper
6. Let beef and onions marinate for 2 -3 hours
7. Skewer beef and onions in alternating pattern
8. Pour some kebab powder in flat dish or on foil
9. Brush uncooked kebab with oil and dip both sides in kebab powder
10. **For oven cooking**: cover baking pan with aluminum foil, brush lightly with oil
11. Place skewered meat on the baking pan and let cook for 20 -25 minutes until meat is cooked; **For grilling**: let cook for 15 - 20 minutes
12. Brush kebabs with oil and dip in some kebab pepper every 5 minutes until cooked

Helpful hints and more:

- As the kebabs are cooking, base them every 3 - 5 minutes with kebab powder until they are cooked
- You can base them using a cooking brush or simply grab end of stick (WEAR GLOVES) and dip both sides in the kebab powder (in bowl or on foil).
- Also base at least once or twice whilst cooking with some oil so as not to dry the meat.
- Kebab pepper is also called Suya.
- This is perfect on its own or with a dish such as Jollof (later chapter).
- OUTSIDE THE BOX - mostly everyone in my high school tried this once! It may seem a little weird at first, but once you try this, you will never go back! Here goes...

  - Take a burger bun and place the kebab in the bun. Hold down the bun tightly and pull on the stick until only the meat is left in the bun. Discard the stick. We call this a "kebab sandwich". Seriously yummy! Goes great with very chilled soda! Mmmmmm...
  - let me know what you think.
  - You can find kebab pepper at your local African grocery store - visit www.africanbiz-byzip.com to find an African grocery store near you.

Fun Fact

When making a phone call to Ghana, the country code is 233

OVEN-BAKED FISH

Makes 4 Servings

Ingredients:

- 2 whole fish (grouper or Tilapia)
- 1 tablespoon of parsley
- 1 tablespoon of garlic paste
- 1 medium onion, finely diced
- 2 tablespoons of black pepper
- 2 tablespoon of white pepper
- 2 tablespoon of fish seasoning
- 2 lemons
- ½ cup of vegetable oil
- 2 tablespoons of salt

Preparation:

1. Clean outside and inside of the fish
2. Grind the garlic and onion together with a blender or food processor
3. Mix the parsley, white pepper and black pepper with the vegetable oil
4. Mix in the ground garlic and onions to the oil mix
5. Rub each fish(inside and outside) with the spiced oil mix
6. Cut 1of the lemons into thin slices and place on each fish
7. Squeeze juice from remaining lemon on each fish
8. Brush fish with a little oil
9. Use a fork to poke a few holes in each fish, wrap each fish in foil
10. Place both fish in the fridge and let them marinate in the spices for about 1 hour
11. Place fish on a baking tray and bake in oven at 350F for about 30 minutes
12. Open up foil and let each fish cook for about another 10 minutes

Helpful hints and more:

- Using a fork to poke holes in the fish allows each fish to be deeply marinated in the spices.
- To make things simpler, you can always have the fish cleaned and scaled when buying it from the grocery store.
- You can mix the spice with some room temperature, salted butter instead of the vegetable oil.
- You can brush each fish with olive oil instead of vegetable oil.
- Instead of fish seasoning, you can also crush two Maggi cubes (shrimp flavor)
- You can place a few slices of salted butter in the fish before baking it in the oven.
- You can also add a ½ tablespoon of ginger paste to the parley mix.
- The fish should be wrapped in foil when baking so that the marinated juices do not evaporate while baking.
- Wrap each fish in a separate foil.
- Test the fish with a toothpick. The fish is cooked when the toothpick comes out clean.

Fun Fact

The Ghanaian flag consists of red, yellow and green horizontal stripes with a black star in the middle of the yellow stripe

FRIED CHICKEN

Makes 8 - 10 servings

Ingredients:

- 4 lbs of chicken thighs or drumsticks
- 2 cups of all-purpose flour
- ½ cup of red pepper powder
- ½ tablespoon of salt
- 1 Maggi crevette
- 2 tablespoons of parsley
- 1 tablespoon of chicken seasoning
- 2 bay leaves
- 1 large white onion
- 1 small-sized ginger root (1 ½ inches long & ½ inch wide)
- vegetable oil (for frying)
- 2 cups of water

Preparation:

1. Wash chicken and place in a pot and season with the chicken seasoning, salt, Maggi cube and bay leaves
2. Puree onion and ginger in a blender and add to the chicken pieces
3. Add the 2 cups of water to the seasoned chicken and let steam on medium-high heat for 30 minutes, until cooked
4. Turn off heat, remove steamed chicken from the cooking pot and place in a bowl; let chicken stock cool
5. Mix flour and red pepper in a separate bowl and slowly add 1 ½ cups of stock to form a batter
6. In another cooking pot, heat up some oil on medium-high for about 10 minutes
7. Take a few cooked chicken pieces, dip them in the batter and place in heated oil
8. Fry chicken for 2 minutes on each side until golden brown.
9. Place fried chicken on plate lined with paper towel

Helpful Hints and more:

- Line plate with paper towel to absorb excess oil from fried chicken
- Another option for a spicier fried chicken is to blend about 2 habanero peppers with the onion and ginger and add to chicken before steaming
- Taste the batter to ensure adequate seasoning before coating the chicken pieces. If you need more spices, add more.
- Make sure that the oil is fully heated before frying
- For every ½ cup of flour , use about 1 cup of stock to form the batter
- Steaming the chicken ensures that the chicken is fully cooked as frying chicken can be a little tricky.
- Steaming also allows for less time that the chicken needs to be fried in all that oil ... low fat fried chicken!

Fun Fact

The Akan calendar runs 40 days

FRIED FISH

Makes 4 servings

Ingredients:

- 4 red snappers
- 1 teaspoon of salt
- 4 tablespoons of ginger paste
- 1 tablespoon of red pepper powder
- 1 crushed Maggi cube (shrimp flavor)
- 1 ½ cups of vegetable oil

Preparation:

1. Clean fish thoroughly
2. Make two deep cuts in each side of each fish
3. Mix ginger paste, red pepper powder and salt
4. Rub spice mix on each side of each snapper and let marinate for 30 minutes
5. Heat oil in deep frying pan on medium heat
6. Deep fry fish for 3 minutes on each side until golden brown

Helpful hints and more:

- To simplify things, make sure the fish is descaled and cleaned before buying at your local grocery store.
- This fried fish goes great with some kenkey and red pepper sauce

Fun Fact

Ghana produces about 17% of the world's cocoa

BEEF & BELL PEPPERS

Makes 4 - 6 servings

Ingredients:

- 3 ½ lbs of lean boneless shoulder steak beef
- 1 medium-sized ginger root (2 ½ inches long & 1 inch wide)
- 2 large white onions
- 1 large green bell pepper, diced
- 1 teaspoon of salt
- ½ cup of red wine vinegar (use a 1/4 cup to marinate beef)
- 4 tablespoons of ketchup
- 1/4 cup of vegetable oil
- 2 Maggi cubes
- 1 tablespoon of chopped garlic
- 3 tablespoons of paprika powder
- 1 tablespoon of crushed red pepper
- 1 tablespoon of basil leaves

Preparation:

1. Cut beef into thin strips
2. Mix beef strips with salt, garlic, 1 tablespoon of paprika and 1/4 cup red wine vinegar
3. Let marinate for about 15 - 20 minutes
4. Wash and peel ginger and grate into a paste
5. Wash and dice green bell peppers
6. Wash and cut onions into rings
7. Heat the vegetable oil on medium heat for about 6 minutes
8. Add onion rings to the heated oil and let fry for about 3 minutes
9. Then stir in the marinated beef; let cook for 20 minutes
10. Add grated ginger, basil, ketchup and 1/4 cup red wine vinegar to the cooking beef
11. After 10 minutes, add the diced bell pepper, paprika and crushed red pepper
12. Let the stew simmer on medium-low heat for about 30 -40 minutes; stir every 15 minutes
13. Add salt to taste

Helpful Hints and more:

- I find that using a wooden spoon for cooking this dish is the best way to go.
- If you do not have access to Maggi cubes, you can always use regular beef bouillon cubes.
- If you are using fresh garlic, use about ½ clove and dice into tiny pieces.
- For a more colorful dish, you can add red and yellow bell peppers.
- This dish can be enjoyed with white rice or even fried rice...and a tall glass of fresh home made lemonade!

Fun Fact

Kumasi is the capital of the Ashanti region

STAPLES

FUFU

Makes 4 servings

Ingredients

- 1 cup Fufu flour
- 2 cups of water

Preparation

1. Boil the 2 cups of water in a cooking pot on medium heat
2. Remove water from heat, add fufu flour and stir with spoon until thoroughly mixed
3. Place mixture back on the medium heat and knead with a wooden spoon for about 4 - 5 minutes until you get a thick, solid consistency.
4. Take it off the stove and let the mix cool for about 3 - 5 minutes
5. Thoroughly wet hands then scoop 1/4 of the fufu ,with a wooden spoon, in your hands and mold into a ball and place in serving bowl
6. Repeat step 5 for the remaining fufu (divide into 3 parts)
7. Serve with soup.

Helpful hints and more:

- Moisten your hands with a little water when molding the fufu.
- You can also keep a small bowl of cold water next to you when molding the fufu so as not to burn yourself.
- Serve fufu with peanut soup, palm nut soup or light soup
- It is traditionally eaten with fingers but a nice, lovely tablespoon will do! Break off a small piece of the fufu, dip it into some soup and swallow.
- You can get fufu flour from any store that sells imported African food products - visit www.africanbizbyzip.com to find an African grocery store near you.
- The traditional method of preparing fufu is by boiling some plantains and yams. They are then placed in a large mortar and pounded with a large pestle to form a soft, smooth doughy substance known as fufu. It is always served with soup.
- You can also mix the fufu flour with the room temperature water and then place on the stove (pre-heated for about 2 minutes).
- You can get a wooden spoon / paddle from your local African grocery store (www.africanbizbyzip.com)

Fun Fact

Kejetia market, in Kumasi, is Ghana's largest open air market

KENKEY

Makes 4 servings

Ingredients

- 2 cups of fermented cornmeal (room temperature)
- aluminum foil or yellow corn husks
- 1 tablespoon vinegar
- 1 cup hot water
- 1 teaspoon salt
- 1 bamboo steamer

Preparation

1. Dampen fermented cornmeal with 2 tablespoons of water to form dough
2. Add vinegar and salt to cornmeal dough
3. Knead dough until it is mixed well, then divide into two pieces
4. Boil 1 cup of water in a cooking pot
5. Slowly add ONE piece of dough into boiling water and cook for 5 minutes on medium heat
6. Take the cooking pot off the stove and combine boiled dough with uncooked piece of dough; knead until mixed well
7. Divide dough into 4 pieces and wrap each in some foil or corn husks
8. Fill a pot with water and bring to boil.
9. Place wrapped pieces of dough in the bamboo steamer and place on top of the pot of boiling water
10. Let it steam cook for 30 - 40 minutes until kenkey is ready

Helpful Hints and more:

- You can get a bamboo steamer at your local Asian grocery store or kitchen section at your local department store.
- If you do not have a bamboo steamer, place uncooked kenkey in a metal sieve (with lid) and place on top of a pot of boiling water and let it steam cook for 30 - 40 minutes.
- To increase the tanginess of your kenkey, you can add an extra ½ tablespoon of vinegar
- To get a sweet and sour taste in your kenkey, add 1 tablespoon of sugar to dough
- You can find fermented cornmeal in the frozen food aisle at your local African grocery store - visit www.africanbizbyzip.com to find a local African grocery store.
- When not in use, always keep the fermented cornmeal in the freezer
- You can also use kenkey cornmeal
- If you do not have an African grocery store available, you can use regular cornmeal (however, you would have to ferment it before cooking, which takes about 6 hours!)
- Kenkey is normally prepared in corn husks but it can be substituted with foil
- Kenkey is normally eaten with red pepper sauce (see recipe for fried yams) and fried or smoked fish (anchovies, Tilapia, grouper).
- It can also be enjoyed with any stew such as chicken stew or garden egg stew

Fun Fact

Ashanti proverb - The ruin of a nation begins in the homes of its people

BANKU

Makes 4 servings

Ingredients

- 4 cups of fermented cornmeal
- 2 cups of water

Preparation

1. Mix the fermented cornmeal with the 2 cups of water in a cooking pot
2. Place the cooking pot on a heated stove and let the cornmeal liquid cook for 20 minutes
3. Stir constantly using a long, wooden pestle or large, wooden spoon
4. The banku should stiffen and become thick as it cooks
5. Let cool for a few minutes then mold cooked banku into 4 equal pieces

Helpful hints and more:

- Banku can be eaten with red pepper sauce (see recipe for fried yams) and fried or smoked fish (grouper, red snapper)
- It can also be enjoyed with any stew such as chicken stew or garden egg stew
- It can also be enjoyed with soup
- **When cooking the banku, add a little water as needed if it becomes too thick to stir**
- You can find fermented cornmeal in the frozen food aisle at your local African grocery store
- When not in use, always keep the fermented cornmeal in the freezer
- If you cannot find fermented corn flour, you can use banku mix (fermented banku flour)
- You can find fermented cornmeal at your local African grocery store - visit www.africanbizbyzip.com to find an African grocery store near you.

Fun Fact

Ashanti Proverb - Rain beats a leopard's skin, but it does not wash out the spots

RICE BALLS

Makes 4 - 6 servings

Ingredients

- 2 cups of white rice
- 4 ½ cups of water
- 1 teaspoon of salt

Preparation

1. Wash rice thoroughly then put in a cooking pot
2. Add 4 ½ cups of water and salt then let rice cook on medium-low heat for 35 minutes
3. Cooked rice should have a soft, moist texture
4. Let cool for about 3 - 5 minutes
5. Scoop rice in a small bowl or container (ramekin)
6. Wet both hands with some water then place rice from bowl into your hands
7. Mold rice into round shape, frequently wetting hands and place in a serving bowl

Helpful hints and more:

- Normally 1 cup of rice is cooked with 1 ½ cups of water but in order to make the rice easy to mold, you need to add a little bit more water to make it stick together
- Rice balls can be eaten with peanut soup, palm nut soup or a combination of both soups
- As you are molding the rice, always wet hands a few times to make molding easier. Keep a small bowl of cool or cold water next to you when molding since the rice is hot. This will cool your hands before you mold the rice.
- WAIT for rice to cool a little before molding as it is HOT! Safety first!
- Place rice balls in a bowl and serve with groundnut (peanut) soup...

Fun Fact

In 1900, the Ashanti Queen mother, Yaa Asantewaa, led the Ashanti rebellion against British colonialism

FRIED RICE

Makes 8 - 10 servings

Ingredients

- 3 cups of jasmine or basmati rice
- 5 large eggs
- 1 medium white onion
- 3 carrot sticks
- 1 cup of green peas
- 1/4 cup vegetable oil or ½ cup of butter
- 2 Maggi cubes
- soy sauce

Preparation

1. Wash rice and put in a cooking pot
2. Add 4 ½ cups of water to rice and boil on medium heat for 20 - 25 minutes until cooked
3. While rice is cooking, dice onions, grate carrots and whisk eggs and place each in a separate bowl
4. In a large frying pan, heat oil or butter
5. Add diced onions and cook for a about 1 minute
6. Stir in whisked eggs till they become scrambled and cooked
7. Crush Maggi cubes and add to scrambled eggs
8. Add in grated carrots and green peas; let cook for about 1 minute
9. Slowly stir in cooked rice and thoroughly mix in with other cooked ingredients
10. Sprinkle in a little soy sauce to the fried rice
11. Let rice simmer on low heat for another 3 - 5 minutes

Helpful hints and more:

- When cooking rice, add some salt to the water to give the cooked rice some taste and therefore, avoid adding too much soy sauce to fried rice.
- If you have a rice cooker available, you can use that to cook your white rice.
- You can also used long-grain rice for this recipe.
- Add enough soy sauce to the fried rice according to your taste of saltiness.

Fun Fact

The largest man-made lake, the Volta lake, is in Ghana

JOLLOF RICE WITH CORNED BEEF

Makes 8 - 10 servings

Ingredients

- 1 can (29oz) of tomato puree
- 2 medium white onions
- 1 orange habanero pepper
- 1 small-sized ginger root (1 ½ inches long & ½ inch wide)
- ½ cup of vegetable oil
- 1 teaspoon nutmeg powder
- 1 can of corned beef
- 2 Maggi cubes
- 3 cups jasmine rice
- 2 tablespoons of salt

Preparation

1. Wash and peel onions; dice 1 of the onions
2. Place other whole onion in blender, add ginger, habanero peppers and tomato puree and blend till even texture
3. Heat oil in cooking pot
4. Add diced onions and let simmer for 3 minutes
5. Add nutmeg and let simmer for 1 minute
6. Pour in blended tomato mix
7. Let mixture cook on medium heat for 20 minutes
8. Crush Maggi cubes and add to cooking pot 10 minutes after adding tomato mix
9. Afer 20 minutes of simmering, add corned beef and let cook for 20 minutes.
10. Add the 2 tablespoons of salt to the sauce
11. Wash rice and add to the sauce
12. Stir well until all the rice is completely mixed with the sauce
13. Let jollof cook for about 45 minutes on low heat; keep lid on cooking pot
14. Stir every 15 minutes so all the rice gets evenly cooked

Helpful hints and more:

- You can use basmati or long-grain rice for this dish.
- Make sure the tomato sauce is cooked before adding the rice!
- Make sure the saltiness of stew is to your liking before adding the rice!
- You can also add some frozen peas and sweet corn to the sauce before adding the rice... makes the dish more colorful
- If you do not want the jollof to be too spicy, only add a ½ of the habanero pepper
- You can also use red pepper powder instead of the habanero pepper
- If you do not have access to the imported red pepper powder, you can blend some chili peppers with the tomatoes or you can use crushed red pepper powder.
- Always keep the lid on the cooking pot. This is especially important when you add the rice because it helps keep the steam inside which helps cook the rice.

Fun Fact

The number to dial for emergency in Ghana is 999 and not 911!

JOLLOF RICE WITH BEEF

Makes 8 - 10 servings

Ingredients

- 1 can (29 oz) of tomato puree
- 2 medium white onions
- 1 orange habanero pepper
- 1 small-sized ginger root (1 ½ inches long & ½ inch wide)
- ½ cup of vegetable oil
- 1 teaspoon nutmeg powder
- 1lb of lean beef
- 2 Maggi cubes
- 3 cups of jasmine rice
- 2 tablespoons of salt

Preparation

1. Wash and peel onions; dice 1 of the onions
2. Place other whole onion in blender, add ginger, habanero pepper and can of tomato puree and blend till even texture
3. Cut and dice beef and place in a cooking pot
4. Add salt and handful of diced onions and let cook on medium-low heat until beef is cooked
5. Heat oil in another cooking pot for 3 -5 minutes
6. Add remaining diced onions to the hot oil and let simmer for 3 minutes on medium heat
7. Add nutmeg and let simmer for 2 minutes
8. Pour in blended tomato mix
9. Let mixture cook on medium heat for 20 minutes
10. Crush Maggi cubes and add to cooking pot after 10 minutes of simmering
11. After 20 minutes of simmering, add cooked beef (and its stock) and let cook for 25 minutes.
12. Add the 2 tablespoons of salt to the sauce
13. Wash rice and add in to stew
14. Stir well until all the rice is completely mixed with the sauce
15. Let jollof cook for about 45 minutes on low heat
16. Stir every 15 minutes so all the rice gets evenly cooked

Helpful hints and more:

- You can also use basmati or long-grain rice for this dish
- Make sure the tomato sauce is cooked before adding the rice!
- **Make sure the saltiness of stew is to your liking before adding the rice**!
- You can also add some frozen peas and corn(thawed) to the sauce before adding the rice... makes the dish more colorful.
- If you do not want the jollof to be too spicy, only add a ½ of habanero pepper
- You can also use red pepper powder instead of the habanero pepper
- If you do not have access to the imported red pepper powder, you can blend some chili peppers with the tomatoes or you can use crushed red pepper powder.
- Always keep the lid on the cooking pot. This is especially important when you add the rice because it helps keep the steam inside which helps cook the rice.

Fun Fact

Visas are required by most non-residents except for ECOWAS members

JOLLOF RICE WITH SARDINES

Makes 8 - 10 servings

Ingredients

- 1 29oz can of tomato puree
- 2 medium white onions
- 1 orange habanero pepper
- 1 small-sized ginger root (1 ½ inches long & ½ inch wide)
- ½ cup of vegetable oil
- 1 teaspoon nutmeg powder
- 10 cans of sardines in tomato sauce (tinapa)
- 2 Maggi cubes
- 3 cups of jasmine rice
- 2 tablespoons of salt

Preparation

1. Wash and peel onions; dice 1 of the onions
2. Place other whole onion in blender, add ginger, habanero pepper and can of tomato puree and blend till even texture
3. Heat oil in cooking pot for 3 minutes on medium heat
4. Add diced onions and let simmer for 3 minutes
5. Add nutmeg and let simmer for 2 minutes
6. Pour in blended tomato mix
7. Let mixture simmer on medium heat for 20 minutes
8. Crush Maggi cubes and add to cooking pot after 10 minutes of simmering
9. After 20 minutes of simmering, add the canned sardines and let cook for 25 minutes.
10. Add the 2 tablespoons of salt to the sauce
11. Wash rice and add in to stew
12. Stir well until all the rice is completely mixed with the sauce
13. Let jollof cook for about 45 minutes on low heat
14. Stir every 15 minutes so all the rice gets evenly cooked

Helpful hints and more:

- You can also use basmati or long-grain rice for this dish
- Make sure the tomato sauce is cooked before adding the rice!
- **Make sure the saltiness of stew is to your liking before adding the rice**!
- You can also add some frozen peas and sweet corn(thawed) to the sauce before adding the rice...makes the dish more colorful
- If you do not want the jollof to be too spicy, only add a ½ teaspoon of red pepper powder
- Add tomato sauce from about 5 cans of the sardines; adding from all the cans will dilute the stew for cooking the rice
- If you do not have access to the imported red pepper powder, you can blend some chili peppers with the tomatoes or you can use crushed red pepper powder.
- Always keep the lid on the cooking pot. This is especially important when you add the rice because it helps keep the steam inside which helps cook the rice.

Fun Fact

ECOWAS = Economic Community of West African States

GARI FOTOR

Makes 10 - 12 servings

Ingredients

- 3 cups of gari
- 1 29oz can of tomato puree
- 2 teaspoons of red pepper powder
- 1 teaspoon of nutmeg powder
- 2 cans of corned beef
- 1 large white onion - dice half and leave other half whole
- ½ cup of vegetable oil
- 2 Maggi cubes
- 2 tablespoons of salt

Preparation

1. Heat oil on medium-high heat for 5 minutes
2. Add diced onion to oil and fry for 3 minutes
3. Stir in pepper powder and nutmeg to frying onions
4. Add 1/4 cup of water to the frying onions and let simmer for 3 minutes
5. Blend tomato puree and other half of onion and add to frying onions
6. Let sauce cook on medium heat for 30 minutes
7. Add corned beef to cooking sauce
8. Let simmer on low heat for about 30 minutes until sauce is cooked
9. Stir in the 2 tablespoons of salt to the sauce
10. Moisten gari with some water and add into sauce
11. Stir until all the gari is covered in sauce and let simmer on low heat for 10 minutes
12. Turn the heat off, but leave gari fotor on stove for 5 - 10 minutes

Helpful hints and more:

- When preparing the sauce, you can use diced lean beef or minced meat instead of corned beef.
- Another way to serve gari fotor is to place 1/4 cup of gari in a bowl, moisten it with some water, add some sauce or stew and stir thoroughly.
- Moistening the gari is important in order to prevent very dry gari fotor.
- Canned corned beef is different from the corned beef used in sandwiches!
- You can also use the recipe for beans stew as your base for gari fotor
- Gari is made of yams and looks like couscous
- It is normally used as a base to eat with stews and sauces
- If you do not have access to the imported red pepper powder, you can blend some chili peppers with the tomatoes or you can use crushed red pepper powder.

Fun Fact

Ghanaian proverb - Do not call the forest that shelters you a jungle

WAACHÉ AND BEEF SAUCE

Makes 8 - 10 servings

Ingredients

- 2 medium size white onions
- 8 large tomatoes or 1 large can (29oz) of tomato puree
- 1 teaspoon of red pepper powder
- ½ cup of vegetable oil
- 2 Maggi cubes
- ½ lb of black-eyed peas (½ the pack)
- 2 ½ cups rice
- 2 waaché leaves (imported)
- 2 lbs of beef (diced)
- 1 tablespoon baking soda
- 4 tablespoons of salt

Preparation

Waaché - rice cooked with black-eyed peas

1. Rinse black-eyed peas
2. Add 4 cups of cold water and let stand overnight
3. Drain and rinse peas
4. Add 6 cups of warm water to rinsed peas
5. Add waaché leaves, 2 tablespoons of salt and baking soda to peas and simmer on medium-low heat, with lid tilted, for 2 ½ hrs
6. Wash rice and add to cooked beans; let cook on low heat until rice is cooked (30 - 40 minutes)

Beef Sauce

7. Place diced beef and 1/4 cup of water in a pot and steam for 20 minutes till cooked
8. In a separate pot, heat vegetable oil for 5 - 7 minutes
9. Add diced onions, Maggi cubes, pepper powder and cooked beef the heated oil and let simmer for 4 minutes
10. Blend tomatoes and add to frying onions; let simmer for 15 minutes
11. Then add ½ cup of water to the cooking sauce
12. Let sauce cook for 30- 40 minutes
13. Add salt to taste
14. Serve with waaché

Helpful hints and more:

- To adjust the level of spiciness, you can add more red pepper powder to beef sauce
- Serve the waaché and sauce with a dash of "gari" and some kele wele
- If you do not have access to the red pepper powder (imported from Ghana), you can blend some chili peppers with the tomatoes or you can use crushed red pepper powder.
- When you add the rice to the cooked beans, make sure there is enough water remaining in the pot to cook the rice (1 ½ cups of water for 1 cup of rice).
- Before adding the rice to the cooked beans, make sure the saltiness of the water is to your liking as that will affect the taste of the rice
- **START** cooking the beef sauce after you leave the beans to simmer for 2 ½ hours.

Fun Fact

Ghanaian proverb - He who cannot dance will say: "The drum is bad."

OTO: YAM VERSION

Makes 4 servings

Ingredients

- half a tuber of yam
- 1/4 cup of palm oil
- 1 tablespoon of salt
- 4 eggs

Preparation

1. Peel and slice yam into pieces then wash them
2. Place washed yam pieces in salted water and boil for 25 minutes till cooked
3. Boil eggs in another cooking pot for about 12 - 15 minutes till well done
4. Drain cooked yam and mash with big spoon until you get a smooth texture
5. Add salt to taste
6. Heat up the palm oil and add to mashed yams
7. Place "oto" into a serving bowl
8. Cut boiled eggs in halves and place on top of "oto" in bowl

Helpful Hints and more:

- Oto is normally eaten to celebrate an event such as a baby's outdooring (naming ceremony of a newborn baby) or one's birthday
- On the morning of birthdays, it is tradition for the person celebrating his or her birthday to eat some oto.
- Yam is one of the staples that is always enjoyed with sauces and soups.
- Add enough salt for your liking. You can use more than the suggested 1 tablespoon.

Fun Fact

In the Akan tradition, the process of asking a family for their daughter's hand in marriage is called "knocking"

OTO: PLANTAIN VERSION

Makes 4 servings

Ingredients

- 2 hard, ripe plantains - diced
- 1 Habanero pepper
- 2 tablespoons of freshly ground peanut paste or unsweetened peanut butter
- 1 small white onion - diced
- 2 tablespoons of palm oil
- 1 cup of roasted peanuts

Preparation

1. Boil plantains in a cooking pot for 30 minutes
2. In another cooking pot, boil onions and peppers
3. When cooked and soft, mash plantains in mortar and pestle till you get smooth texture
4. Puree onion, peppers and peanut paste till you get even texture
5. Add peanut mixture to cooled mashed plantains and mix thoroughly
6. Add a little palm oil (optional) to the oto until evenly mixed
7. Garnish oto with roasted peanuts and enjoy!!!

Helpful hints and more:

- Use"just ripened" plantains for this recipe.
- The plantain should be yellow and very firm
- To test when plantains are cooked, pierce lightly with a fork or knife...it should be tender when pierced.
- You have to mash plantains immediately after they are cooked so they are soft enough to mash
- Use at least a 9" wide granite (stone) mortar and a 7" wooden pestle.
- You can also mash the plantains in any glass bowl using a large wooden spoon.
- Oto is normally eaten to celebrate an event such as a baby's outdooring (naming ceremony of a newborn baby) or one's birthday
- Adding palm oil is optional

Fun Fact

During "knocking", the groom-to-be and his family visit his soon to be in-laws with gifts

FRIED RED PLANTAINS

Makes 4 servings

Ingredients

- 4 ripe plantains (yellow skin, firm)
- 3 cups of vegetable oil
- 1 teaspoon of salt

Preparation

1. Wash and peel plantains
2. Cut across horizontally then cut each into very thick diagonal slices
3. Wash and place in bowl of water; add 1 teaspoon of salt to water
4. Pour vegetable oil into a pot and place on medium-high heat for 10 minutes
5. Fry plantains for 2 ½ minutes on each side until golden and brown
6. Place on sheet lined with paper napkins
7. Repeat process with remaining uncooked plantains

Helpful hints and more:

- Fried plantains are normally eaten with beans stew.
- Fried plantains can also be eaten by itself or with a dish such as Jollof.
- Ripe plantains are also called red plantains
- Since beans stew is prepared with palm oil, which is also red, the combination of fried, ripe plantains and beans stew is called "RED RED"
- OUTSIDE THE BOX: I also like to heat up some vegetarian baked beans with some palm oil and use it as a sauce for my fried, red plantains

Fun Fact

If the "knocking" is accepted, the families start making plans for the wedding

ROASTED RED PLANTAINS

Makes 4 servings

Ingredients

- 4 ripe plantains (yellow skin, firm)
- roasted peanuts

Preparation

1. Wash and peel plantains
2. Cut across horizontally and then into thick diagonal slices
3. Place plantains on foil
4. Preheat oven at 400F and bake plantains for 30 minutes **or**
5. Place plantains on a grill for 20 minutes

Helpful hints and more:

- Dip roasted plantains in roasted peanuts before eating...simply lovely!
- When roasting plantains on a grill, remember to cook each side for about 10 - 12 minutes until golden and brown
- You can also roast plantains on a charcoal grill or a small counter-top grill

Fun Fact

Ghanaian proverb - No one tests the depth of a river with both feet

BAKED GOODIES

DOUGHNUTS

Makes 4 servings

Ingredients

- 1 ½ cups of all-purpose flour
- 1 tablespoon of baking powder
- ½ cup of sugar
- ½ teaspoon salt
- 3 fl oz whole milk
- 1 egg
- 2 teaspoons of nutmeg powder
- 1 tablespoon of vanilla extract
- vegetable oil (for frying)

Preparation

1. Mix sugar, baking powder, salt and nutmeg with flour in a mixing bowl
2. In another bowl, add milk and vanilla extract to egg and mix well
3. Slowly add milk mixture to flour ; use hand-mixer to slowly mix ingredients
4. Mix until texture is smooth and even
5. Heat oil in a deep pot ,on medium-high heat, for 7 - 10 minutes
6. Scoop pieces of dough using a small ice-cream scoop (with lever) and drop in hot oil
7. Fry for 1 ½ minutes on each side
8. Place doughnuts on sheet lined with paper towel (to absorb excess oil)
9. Repeat steps 6,7,8 with remaining dough.

Helpful hints and more:

- Heat oil on medium heat but do not fry dough until oil is fully heated
- To test if oil is heated, put a small amount of batter in the oil... if you see lots of little bubbles, then the oil is fully heated
- You can use other extracts instead of vanilla...almond is usually good too!
- For a "not-too-thick" doughnut, use 1 cup of flour instead of 1 ½ cups.
- Using a SMALL scoop is important because bigger scoops will cause the outside of the doughnuts to cook faster than the inside and you will end up with burnt, undercooked doughnuts!
- You can also use a tablespoon to drop the dough into the hot oil.
- If coating the doughnuts with sugar or dipping in melted chocolate, you can use 1/3 cup of sugar instead of ½ cup as indicated in the ingredient list.
- If the oil is not hot enough, the doughnuts will absorb too much oil
- If the oil is too hot, the doughnuts will burn on the outside and be undercooked on the inside

Fun Fact

Soccer (football) is the most popular sport in Ghana

MEAT PIE

Makes 4 servings

Ingredients

PASTRY

- 3 cups all-purpose flour
- 1 cup of salted butter or margarine
- 1 tablespoon of nutmeg
- 1 ½ tablespoons of baking powder
- 2 fl oz of vegetable oil
- 1/4 cup whole milk or evaporated milk
- 1 egg (beat and use as egg wash)

FILLING

- ½ lb ground lean beef
- 1 medium white onion - diced
- 1 teaspoon of salt
- 1/4 cup of vegetable oil
- 1 teaspoon of black pepper

Preparation:

1. Combine flour, nutmeg and baking powder in a bowl
2. Mix in butter or margarine until mixture resembles bread crumbs
3. Slowly pour in vegetable oil and mix in with the flour
4. Then slowly pour in the milk to the flour mixture and mix well till dough is formed
5. Cover dough with plastic wrap and put in fridge for 1 hour
6. Meanwhile, heat 1/4 cup of oil in frying pan and fry the diced onion on medium heat for 3 minutes
7. Season ground beef with salt and add to frying onions for 10 - 15 minutes until cooked
8. After 1 hour is up, take dough out of fridge
9. Separate dough into 4 equal pieces and roll out flat and cut into a circle using large round cookie cutter
10. Place 2 tablespoons of the filling on one-half of each flattened piece of dough
11. Brush edges with egg wash, fold over and seal each pie by pressing a fork along the edges
12. Brush each pie with egg wash and bake at 400F for 20 minutes

Helpful hints and more:

- Season the filling according to your tastes - you can use, minced meat or even ground chicken meat!
- You can also use canned corned beef as a filling.
- You can use more filling per pie if desired.
- If you do not have a cookie cutter, you can use an object of similar size and material that can cut out the dough.
- When brushing egg over uncooked pie, use a cooking brush to prevent over basing of egg on the dough.
- Make sure to brush top side of pie with the egg wash before baking.
- Egg wash - when an egg is beaten and a small quantity of water (1 tablespoon) is added to it. It gives the pie a nice shine.

Fun Fact

The use of the left hand to eat or greet someone is considered disrespectful

ACHOMO

Makes 4 servings

Ingredients

- 2 cups all-purpose flour
- ½ teaspoon of baking powder
- ½ teaspoon of cinnamon
- ½ teaspoon of nutmeg
- 1/4 cup of salted butter (½ stick of butter)
- 1/4 cup of water
- 1/4 cup of sugar

Preparation

1. Mix baking powder, cinnamon and butter with flour until mix resembles bread crumbs
2. In a separate bowl, mix sugar with water
3. Add sugar water to flour mix until it turns doughy
4. Knead the dough for 3 minutes
5. Roll dough out flat (½ inch thick) and cut into squares
6. Heat oil in a cooking pot, on medium heat for 5 - 7 minutes
7. Place some cut dough pieces in the hot oil and fry for 5 -7 minutes until golden brown
8. Remove "achomo"and place on paper sheet
9. Repeat steps 7 and 8 with remaining dough pieces

Helpful hints and more:

- When rolling the dough, flatten into about ½ inch thick.
- Cut dough into equal pieces so frying time will be the same for all
- To adjust the taste of the pastry you can adjust the amount of sugar added
- Store in an airtight container and keep in a fridge - this will help it last longer!

Fun Fact

100 pesewas equal 1 cedi

ROCK BUN

Makes 6 - 8 buns

Ingredients

- 2 cups of all-purpose flour
- ½ cup of salted butter (1 stick of butter)
- 1 tablespoon of baking powder
- 1 egg (beaten)
- 1/4 cup of sugar
- ½ cup of evaporated milk

Preparation

1. Place the 2 cups of flour in a mixing bowl
2. Add in sugar and baking powder
3. Mix in butter until flour resembles bread crumbs
4. In a cup, beat egg and add evaporated milk
5. Slowly pour in egg mixture to flour and mix until even texture dough forms
6. Tear off a piece of the dough and shape into a circle or desired bun-shape
7. Repeat step 7 until you have about 6 to 8 buns
8. Place foil on a baking tray
9. Place buns on the baking tray and place in preheated oven (400F)
10. Bake rock buns for 16 minutes

Helpful Hints and More:

- You can also use margarine to mix into the flour
- You can use your hand or you can use a cake mixer to mix in the ingredients for this recipe.
- If the dough seems dry, add 2 to 4 tablespoons of evaporated milk to the mix.
- You can also use fresh milk (whole or 2%) instead of evaporated milk.
- You can also put raisins or any dried fruit of your choice...or even chocolate morsels!
- For a sweeter rock bun, use ½ cup of sugar instead of 1/4 cup.
- To get a softer texture before eating, you can microwave the buns for 5 - 10 seconds.

Fun Fact

Bauxite is one of Ghana's natural resources

POUND CAKE

Makes 1 pound cake

Ingredients

- 3/4 cup sugar
- 1 cup salted butter (2 sticks butter)
- 4 eggs
- 2 cups all-purpose flour
- 2 teaspoons baking powder
- 1 teaspoon vanilla extract

Preparation

1. Beat sugar and butter with an electric hand mixer for 4 - 5 minutes until you get a fluffy texture
2. Add in eggs, one at a time until texture is smooth
3. Add baking powder to flour and slowly add in to butter mix
4. Add vanilla extract to cake mix
5. Butter a loaf baking pan and scoop in cake mixture
6. Bake at 350F for 1 hour
7. Let cake cool for about 20 minutes and cut into slices

Helpful hints and more:

- You can substitute vanilla extract with almond extract
- This recipe makes only one loaf of pound cake so if you have 2 pans, simply double the ingredients.
- When adding in the flour, reduce the speed of your mixer to prevent the flour from flying everywhere.
- Depending on your sweet tooth, you can change the quantity of sugar by using a 1/4 cup less sugar or a 1/4 cup more sugar.
- To vary the flavor of the cake, use different extracts (almond, orange, etc) as well as using additions like raisins, dried cranberries, etc.
- Sift a little powdered sugar on cake before serving
- Another way to enjoy this pound cake is to serve it with some Bird's Eye Custard (imported - international aisle of your grocery store or local African store). You can buy the already made version one or you can cook it yourself. Make sure the custard is slightly chilled and pour it on the serving plate before placing the sliced cake.

Fun Fact

In Ghana, Santa Claus is called "Father Christmas"

SWEETS & NIBBLES

NKATI CAKE (PEANUT TOFFEE)

Makes 4 - 6 servings

Ingredients

- 1 cup of roasted peanuts
- 1 cup of sugar
- 1/3 cup of evaporated milk

Preparation

1. Chop peanuts into little pieces with knife or food processor
2. Pour the sugar in a pan and cook on low heat for 10 minutes until sugar is completely melted
3. Pour in evaporated milk then chopped peanuts and mix until all the peanuts are coated
4. Pour peanut toffee on a wooden cutting board
5. Spread out flat with a long knife or a small rolling pin
6. Cut into squares or preferred shapes.

Helpful hints and more:

- Do not over chop peanuts if using a food processor or they will turn into powder
- Make sure you roll out toffee as flat as possible and cut before it gets cold because then it would be hard
- Try and cut into bite size pieces if possible because it hardens when it cools and it is easier to eat because you can just pop them in your mouth as supposed to biting it off a big piece
- Please do not use low-fat or fat free evaporated milk!

Fun Fact

During Christmas, people visit friends and family and take along baked goods and other food items instead of buying gifts in stores

KUBÉ CAKE (COCONUT TOFFEE)

Makes 4 - 6 servings

Ingredients

- 3 cups shredded coconut
- 3/4 cup sugar
- 1/3 cup of salted butter

Preparation

1. Heat sugar on medium-low heat for 10 minutes until completely melted
2. Add butter to melted sugar
3. Stir until all butter is melted
4. Lower heat and pour in shredded coconut
5. Mix until all coconut pieces are coated
6. Pour onto plate or cutting board and mold into balls
7. Place in fridge and let cool so molded coconut toffee can set
8. Enjoy!

Helpful hints and more:

- If you are using fresh coconuts, break shell and remove the white meat from the shell; then grate coconut meat into tiny, thin slices
- You can get coconuts from your local grocery store
- If you cannot get any fresh coconuts, you can use store-ready shredded coconuts - that's the simplest way!
- Do not use HIGH heat when melting the sugar or else it will burn and give the toffee a bitter taste!
- If you want to eat them right away, place them in the fridge for about 5 - 10 minutes
- If it's for a party, make sure you them out of the fridge a few minutes before serving so the toffee can reach room temperature

Fun Fact

Fishermen in Ghana are superstitious and do not go fishing on Tuesdays!

MILK TOFFEE

Makes 4 - 6 servings

Ingredients

- 1 can of condensed milk

Preparation

1. Heat frying pan on medium heat for 5 minutes
2. Pour in condensed milk and turn down the heat a little
3. Stir mixture slowly until it turns brown and semi-solid
4. Pour onto plate / parchment paper and mold into preferred shapes (cylinder, squares, balls)
5. Let cool and then eat!

Helpful hints and more:

- Do not eat toffee when it is HOT as you can burn yourself!
- There is really no name for this sweet; we just refer to it as condensed milk toffee!
- It hardens when it cools, so the preferred method of eating it is just sucking it...like a hard candy!
- Seriously delicious!!!!!!

Fun Fact

Timber is one of Ghana's natural resources

PLANTAIN CHIPS

Makes 4 servings

Ingredients

- 2 green plantains
- vegetable oil (3 - 4 cups)
- 1 tablespoon of salt
- additional salt (to sprinkle)

Preparation

1. Wash and peel plantains
2. Cut plantains into very thin slices
3. Wash and place sliced plantains in a bowl of water; add 1 tablespoon of salt to water
4. Heat oil on medium-high heat for about 6 minutes
5. Fry plantain slices for 5 - 7 minutes on each side
6. Place plantain chips on a plate lined with paper napkins
7. Repeat steps 5 and 6 with remaining uncooked plantains
8. Sprinkle salt on chips for taste (optional)
9. Enjoy!

Helpful hints and more:

- Make sure oil is hot enough before frying plantains in order to avoid them absorbing too much oil whilst cooking
- Salt is normally added to the water so the plantains can absorb some of the salt before being fried...this reduces the need to add more salt after it is cooked
- For sweeter plantain chips, you can use very firm, just-ripened plantains ...the plantains should be turning yellow.

Fun Fact

Manganese is one of Ghana's natural resources

FRUIT SALAD

Makes 4 servings

Ingredients

- 1 medium pineapple
- 2 medium mangoes
- 2 medium papayas
- 2 large bananas

Preparation

1. Wash and dice pineapple
2. Wash and dice mango and papayas
3. Peel and dice bananas
4. Place all diced fruit in bowl and serve

Helpful hints and more:

- You can wash and dice the pineapple, mango and papaya ahead of time
- Only add banana to fruit salad when it is about to be served because banana will start turning brownish if left out for too long.
- You can use as many of each fruit as you want.

Fun Fact

Ghana is a tropical country on the West coast of Africa

Measurements / Conversions

DRY MEASUREMENTS

1oz = 28.35g = 7 teaspoons
4 g = 1 teaspoon
8g = 1 tablespoon
½ cup = 40g
1 cup = 80g
1 lb = 16oz = 454g

BUTTER / SHORTENING

4 oz butter / margarine = ½ cup of butter / margarine
8 tablespoons of butter = ½ cup of butter / margarine
1 lb of butter = 2 cups of butter

LIQUID MEASUREMENTS

½ teaspoon = 2.5ml
1 teaspoon = 5ml
1 tablespoon = 15ml
1 tablespoon = 3 teaspoons
1 fl oz = 30ml
½ cup = 120ml
1 pint = 2 cups = 480ml
1 quart = 4 cups = 960 ml
1 gallon = 4 quarts = 3.84L

OVEN TEMPERATURE

	Celsius	Fahrenheit
Cool	90	200
Slow	150	300
Moderate	180	350
Hot	200	400

CONVERSIONS

1 fl oz (US) = 1.0408 (UK) fl oz
1 pint(=16fl oz) = 0.8327 pt (UK)
1 pint (dry measurement) = 0.9689 pt (UK)

GLOSSARY OF UNCOMMON INGREDIENTS

ginger root -
root used as a seasoning to spice up many dishes from sauces to soups

plantains -
look like bananas but are totally different. They cannot be eaten raw and hence have to be cooked via boiling, frying or roasting. Both ripe (yellow skin) and unripe (green) versions of plantains are used in everyday cooking (etoh, fufu, kele wele, fried plantain chips).

palm nut paste -
made from the fruit of the palm tree. It is made by boiling the palm fruit and extracting the juices from the skin. This is used in making palm nut soup.

palm oil -
form of edible vegetable oil from the fruit of the palm nut tree. It should not be confused with palm kernel oil which is oil from the seed of the palm tree. Palm oil is liquid but also turns semi-solid at room temperature so do not panic if you look in the pantry and your palm oil looks a little stiff!

garden eggs -
this is an African eggplant. It is called a garden egg because of its shape, size and color… it resembles an egg!

dried fish -
in Ghana, fish(herring, cod , haddock) is normally dried or smoked in order to preserve the fish for future use. It is used in stews and soups.

canned corned beef -
this is totally different from the cured or boiled version of corned beef in making sandwiches! It can be used in making sandwiches too but we normally used it to make dishes such as Jollof or corned beef stew.

fufu flour -
flour made from dried and processed plantains, cassava and yam.

kenkey cornmeal -

made from corn which has been fermented and processed into white flour. Used in making starch staples such as kenkey and banku.

koko flour

made from corn which has been fermented and processed. Used to make porridge called koko.

African yam -

a vegetable tuber with rough brown skin. It is eaten by removing the skin and cooking the white "meat" of the tuber. It can be boiled and eaten with a stew or fried as a snack. It is also used in the preparation of fufu (when cooking from scratch and not with fufu flour) by pounding it with boiled plantains until a smooth texture is formed.

Kebab pepper -

a spicy powder mix made from peanut powder, powdered pepper, ginger, garlic and shrimps. Used on coating kebabs to give it its wonderful, spicy texture and flavor. Also known as "suya".

Serrano pepper

small green peppers that change to orange then red as they mature.

nutmeg -

it is the actual seed of the nutmeg plant and is used as spice in many dishes in Ghana such as sauces as well as baking. It is sold in its nut form as well as powder form. When bought in nut form, it can be used by grating it down to powder form and using a little to give the food a unique flavor.

Cocoyam leaves (kontomire)

these are the leaves of the cocoyam tuber. The leaves are called "kontomire" and used in making spinach stew. This is sort of our version of spinach.

condensed milk -

this is a condensed evaporated milk and used in making sweets and flans (creme caramel).

salad cream -

it is a yellowish condiment...looks like mayonnaise but it is used in salads. It also goes great as a spread when making chicken sandwiches!

gari -

it is made from the cassava root. It looks like couscous but that's where the similarity ends. It is easy to store and can be eaten as a base with stews or as an actual dish (gari fotor).

red pepper powder -

powder version of red chili peppers from Ghana. It is imported and can be found at your local African grocery stores.

cassava -

it is a long root with rough brown skin surrounding white flesh (kind of like yams). It has to be cooked to be edible and is used in preparing many dishes such as fufu; it can be boiled and eaten with stews or fried and eaten as a snack.

red onions -

have purplish skin unlike "regular" onions which have white or yellowish skins. Normally used in Ghanaian dishes such as salads because of its slightly sweet taste.

Fried red plantains
with Bean Stew

Fufu

Jollof Rice

Kebabs with a dash of Kebab Pepper

Kele Wele - spicy, fried red plantains

Peanut Soup

Plantain Chips

Waache

GHANAIAN NAMES

DAY	FEMALE	MALE
Monday	Adwoa / Adjoa	Kwadjo / Kojo
Tuesday	Abena	Kwabena
Wednesday	Akua	Kwaku / Kweku
Thursday	Yaa	Yaw
Friday	Afua	Kofi
Saturday	Ama / Amma	Kwame / Kwamena
Sunday	Akosua	Kwasi / Kwesi

* For example, if you are female and were born on a Monday, then your Ghanaian name would be Adwoa.

PRONUNCIATIONS!

Abé (palm nut)

pronounced "Ah-beh". The AH is a quick, short sound and the BEH is like the be in best.

Abenkwan (palm nut soup)

pronounced "Ah-ben-kwain". The AH is a quick, short sound. The BEN is like the ben in benjamin. The N in KWAIN should be almost silent.

Achomo

pronounced "Ah-cho-mo". The AH is a quick, short sound. The CHO is like the cho in chocolate.

nkati cake (peanut toffee)

Pronounced "In-ka-tti cake". Cake is cake... The IN is a short, quick sound, almost like making a sound for the letter "n". The TTI is like the ti in till.

nkatikwan (peanut soup)

Pronouonced "in-katti-kwain".The IN is a short, quick sound, almost like making a sound for the letter "n". The TTI is like the ti in till. The N in KWAIN should be almost silent.

kubé(coconut)

Pronounced "ku-bay". The KU is like the cou in coup .

kelé welé

Pronounced "Keh-lay Weh-lay".

kor kor (plantain)

Pronounced "kor kohr". The first KOR is like the co in coffee. The second KOR is said in the same manner as you would claw.

koko (porridge)

Pronounced "ko-ko". The KO is like the co in coat.

tatalé (plantain pancake)

Pronounced "Tah-tah-ley". The LEY is like the la in late.

shitor (pepper sauce)
Pronounced "Shii - toh". The TOH is like the to in toddler.

kontomiré (spinach)
Pronounced "Kon-to-mray". The TO is like the to in toll.

jollof
Pronounced "Joh-lof". The JOH is like the jo in jostle. The LOF is like the lof in loft.

waaché-
Ponounced "Waa-chay". The CHAY is like the cha in chase.

gari
Pronounced "Gaa-rii".

oto
Pronounced "Eh- toh. The EH is like ae in aeroplane. The TOH is like the to in toy.

omo tuo (rice balls)
Pronounced "Omu-twoh". The O in OMU can be silent.

kenkey
Pronounced"Ken-key". The KEN sounds like the word cane. The KEY is like the ca in cake.

Adwoa / Adjoa
Pronounced "A-jwa". The "DW" or "DZ" in Ghanaian names is always pronounced like a "J".

ABOUT THE AUTHOR

Sandra Amoako was born and raised in Accra, Ghana. She attended Ghana International School and went on to Bucknell University where she graduated with a Bachelor of Science in Business Administration and minors in Economics and French.

Sandra has always loved to cook and write and spends some of her time cooking for friends and family as well as writing short stories and poetry. Her passion for food continued from high school throughout college (international food fairs). After graduating from Bucknell University, Sandra's passion for cooking and writing remained and she decided to combine her two passions and write her first cookbook, " Akwaaba: A Taste of Ghana."

In her cookbook, "Akwaaba: A Taste of Ghana", Sandra shares many recipes of Ghanaian cuisine and hopes it will be a gateway for food lovers worldwide to make and enjoy Ghanaian cuisine.

ORDERING

ONLINE	MAIL (please include check with order)
www.alikobooks.com	AlikoBooks 491 Baltimore Pike, #447, Springfield, PA 19064

Ordered by:

Name
Address
City
State/ Zip
Phone
Email address

Sales tax:	Please add 6% for products shipped to Pennsylvania addresses
Mail:	$5.98 for first book and $1.99 for each additional book (US Domestic)
	$8.98 for first book and $2.99 for each additional book (Canada)
	$13.98 for first book and $2.99 for each additional book (International)

Quantity	Unit Price		Total
	x $19.95	=	

Merchandise Total:	$
Shipping Charges:	$
Sales Tax (6 %):	$
Grand Total:	$

INDEX

A

B

C

D

E

F

G

H

I

J

K

L

M

N

O

P

R

S

T

V

W

Y